# I Refuse to Choose

## The Best of Both Worlds

by Melissa Montero

# mixedessence

Copyright 2018 by Melissa Montero

First edition published June 2018
All production design are trademarks of Melissa Montero

Print Paperback ISBN: 978-0-578-59261-9

For information regarding bulk purchases of this book, digital purchase and special discounts, please contact the author

~To my three beautiful children Isaiah, Jose Jr. and Mayah for keeping me on my toes.


~To my husband for encouraging me to follow my dreams.

From the moment she woke up, Mayah was bursting with excitement. She sprang out of bed and headed towards the bathroom.

As she brushed her teeth, she saw someone walk past the bathroom door.

"**Papi! Papi!** Guess what today is?" Mayah said.

"**¿Que Quieres mi Amor?**" asked **Papi.**

"We have social studies!" Mayah replied excitedly.

"I can't wait until you come home and tell me all about it," said **Papi**.

Mayah could hardly keep still as her mom tried to brush her hair into her favorite ponytail.

"Mommy, *por favor* hurry; I don't want to be late for school!" said Mayah.

As Mayah headed towards the door, Mommy and **Papi** stood there, eagerly waiting for her to kiss them goodbye.

"Mayah, where are our ***besos y abrazos***?" asked **Papi**.

"The bus is coming, **Papi**," said Mayah.

"Not before I get my ***besos***!" said **Papi**.

"Alllrrrigght," said Mayah as she gave **Papi** a kiss.

"***Adios mi hija***," said **Papi**.

"Love you, princess!" yelled her mom as Mayah scurried out the door.

As the yellow school bus approached the school, Mayah was thankful she sat at the front of the bus. Now she would be first in line!

"What are you smiling about, Mayah?" asked Samantha.

"She is always smiling!" Lee answered as they exited the bus.

"Mrs. Anderson said that she had a big announcement to make today!" said Samantha.

"I have no idea what it's going to be … but I have been waiting all weekend to find out," said Mayah.

As they entered the social studies class, Mayah hurried to her seat, eager to see what the big announcement was.

"Good morning, class," said Mrs. Anderson. "Today, we are going to talk about our project on different cultures. All week, we will learn about different cultures, and on Friday, we will end our unit with student presentations. Each one of you will get 5 minutes to present your culture to the class."

Mayah loved talking in front of the class, so she was very excited.

But when Mrs. Anderson placed a paper on her desk, Mayah's smile instantly turned into a look of concern.

"What's wrong?" Sophia asked.

Mayah just shrugged her shoulders and slipped the paper into her backpack. She could feel the tears welling up in her eyes, and she wished that she could just disappear.

As she looked around the room, all the other kids were talking about what they were going to wear and what they would say.

Mayah just put her head on her desk for what seemed like forever.

Finally, the bell rang! Mayah ran out of the class before anyone else had a chance to ask her what was wrong.

*Papi* stood at the bus stop, waiting for Mayah to run off the bus as she always did.

Today, Mayah was the last one off the bus. Her head hanging low.

"*Hola*, princess, how was school ... how was social studies?" *Papi* said.

Mayah reached into her backpack and handed over the paper that Mrs. Anderson handed out.

*Papi* read the assignment from Mayah's teacher, and when they made it in the house, he handed the assignment over to Mommy.

"Why the long face, Mayah?" What are you so worried about?" asked Mommy.

"I don't know what box to choose," Mayah said as she burst into tears.

They have:

☐ Black/African American          ☐ Native American

☐ White          ☐ Chinese

☐ Asian          ☐ Pacific Islander

☐ Hispanic or Latino

"I understand your concern, princess. But this is not a time to cry but to celebrate!" Mommy said.

"Mommy, how can I celebrate when I don't know what to do? You are African American, and **Papi** is Puerto Rican. I know that means I am both, but what box do I choose?" Mayah asked, looking confused.

"It's a time to celebrate how special and unique God made you. You are a beautiful, talented, smart, loving, caring young lady, and that is why you should celebrate."

"Never allow anyone to make you feel like you must choose one culture or the other." Mommy said.

"You are blessed to celebrate both your Hispanic and African American cultures.

Always be proud of who you are, sweetie."

"You are right, Mommy," Mayah said as she wiped her tears away.

"We can't wait to see your project," said *Papi*.

Mayah grabbed some magazines, scissors, glue, a poster board and her markers as she hurried up the steps to begin her project.

The next morning, as Mommy and **Papi** prepared Mayah's breakfast, they heard her feet hit the floor, and off she went.

"Mayah is back," **Papi** said. She came running down the steps with a poster board secured with a rubber band.

She had on a beautiful outfit that she created herself to represent both cultures.

I refuse to choose!

Once Mayah arrived at Mrs. Anderson's class, she could not wait until it was her turn.

After Lee completed his presentation, Mrs. Anderson said: "Mayah, it's your turn."

Mayah removed the rubber band from her poster and walked toward the front of the class.

She turned to face the class and opened her poster board.

Mayah said, "This project was to choose one culture and complete a project on how it's important to you.

"Well, I am both Puerto Rican and African American. As you can see on my poster, both cultures are special and a part of who I am. I will not choose one ... so I made a puzzle piece for the American flag and the Puerto Rican flag and put it together.

"This means since my Mommy is African American, and my *Papi* is Puerto Rican, I have THE BEST OF BOTH WORLDS."

Mrs. Anderson started clapping, and the class stood and joined in.

Mayah's Mommy and *Papi* had quietly entered in through the back door. They were beaming with pride.

# Spanish Glossary

1. Papi: Daddy
2. Que Quieres Mi Amor: What do you want my love
3. Beso/s: Kisses
4. y: and
5. Abrazos: hugs
6. Hola: Hello
7. Por Favor: Please
8. Adios mi hija: Goodbye my daughter

www.ingramcontent.com/pod-product-compliance
Lightning Source LLC
LaVergne TN
LVHW070348090426
835511LV00029B/68